Non-ficti

Voyage

3

Series Advisers

Shirley Bickler and Raewyn Hickey

Contents

OXFORD

UNIVERSITY PRESS

The Naturalist's Tale

Carol Bruce, a naturalist, is spending 6 months on a small island working for the New Zealand Department of Conservation. In this magazine article, Carol describes a typical day on Stephen's Island, which is off the northern tip of New Zealand's South Island.

A day in the life...

My day starts around 6.30 a.m. searching for tuataras before they head for their burrows to sleep during the heat of the day. Tuataras like cold, damp conditions and will die if their body temperature reaches over 27°C. If I am lucky and find one, I trap it in a net, tag it with a band around its front foot, take a blood sample, then release it. The tuataras I catch are about 40 cm to 60 cm long and can weigh anything from 300g to 1kg.

At about 7.30 a.m. I check the rain gauge to measure any rainfall over the past 24 hours, and record the maximum and minimum temperatures. At present I am collecting blood samples in order to study the immune system of a rare reptile, the tuatara. Tuataras once lived all over New Zealand but are now found on only 32 islands around the coast. Scientists from around the world are interested in the tuatara, because it is the only remaining member of a type of dinosaur which became extinct about 60 million years ago.

Carol's husband holding a tuatara

Supplies arrive by boat

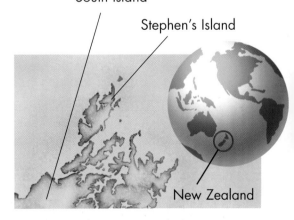

New Zealand South Island

Stephen's Island

New Zealand

Map showing Carol's location

The tuatara is an endangered species.

At 8 o'clock I contact the base in Picton to let them know I am alive and well and then have breakfast. I soak oatmeal at night and feed it to a seagull and a pair of pigeons which turn up every morning. After breakfast I usually prepare the dough for the bread maker, so I can have hot bread for lunch.

I ring the meteorological centre at 9 o'clock to give them the data from the rain and temperature gauges. My recordings help them forecast the weather.

I spend the morning checking the blood samples. After lunch, I might write reports or send emails. If the day is sunny, I might work in my tiny vegetable garden, or go fishing.

I usually have a nap at about 4 o'clock because I have to go out and hunt for more tuataras from about 10 o'clock at night until around 2 a.m.

An email to friends

In this email to friends, Carol recounts some of the problems she has had in the last few weeks.

Delete   Reply   Reply All   Forward   Print

From: c.bruce@tuatara.nz
To: jean-and-chris@backhome.nz
Subject: Life on Stephen's Island
Sent: Tues 29 January 2006 13:15:34

Hi Jean and Chris,

The boat came yesterday, bringing the mail and the groceries. Thanks for the bread maker. It will make my day so much easier. I nearly didn't get any parcels. The mail and supplies have to be unloaded on to a little trolley, which is winched up a railway line to the top of the cliff. Then I load them on to a trailer behind the 4-wheel motorbike to drive the kilometre to the house. Yesterday, near the top, the wire rope snapped. The trolley rolled backwards, gathering speed until it was roaring down the line towards the sea. Fifty metres from the bottom it derailed, spilling its load through the bush and into the gully. Fortunately, everything I had ordered had been well packed. The trolley is demolished and the rails will need repairing. I can see I will be lugging supplies up the cliff for months.

photo1.jpeg

4

You remember I told you I had to get used to having a wind-powered generator for electricity? Last month we had some very strong gales. One morning I found the generator had blown itself to bits! Which, of course, left me with no electricity. Luckily I have a gas cooker, and lots of candles. Thankfully at the same time, the Department was in the process of installing solar power. There were only three days of work left, so I didn't have to wait long.

For the past month there have been six men hunting for deer in the hills. They radio me each night between 7 and 8 o'clock to let me know everything is all right. Last night one of them asked me to sing a poem he had written, to his wife. When I had finished, she cried and said it was the most romantic thing he had ever done.

Take care,

Carol

photo2.jpeg

The Hamilton Frog

A report on the conservation of the Hamilton frog on Stephen's Island, New Zealand

Dr Raymond Hill

Science and Research Division
Department of Conservation, Wellington

Stephen's Island, which covers an area of 2.6 square kilometres off the northern tip of the South Island of New Zealand, is internationally important for nature conservation. It is noted especially for its population of a rare reptile, the tuatara. However, our research has concentrated on possibly the rarest frog in the world, the Hamilton frog, which is found nowhere else in the world.

Description

Leiopelma hamiltoni (the Hamilton frog) is the most critically endangered of all the New Zealand native frogs. It was first listed as endangered on 2 June 1970. Since then, the total population has dwindled to fewer than 300 individuals, of which about 240 are adult. The Hamilton frog belongs to an ancient species which originated 200 million years ago. It is nocturnal, has no ears and does not croak. The frogs do not have a tadpole stage; instead, fully developed froglets hatch from the eggs. The frog is believed to have a lifespan of around 23 years.

The Hamilton frog

Habitat

Stephen's Island is frequently covered in cloud which helps maintain damp conditions. The entire population of the species was discovered in a single rock stack near the summit, where the ground is suitably moist for the frogs to lay their eggs. The narrow crevices between the rocks provide shade.

Hamilton frogs require damp, shady conditions.

Threats

The species faces threats from drought, extreme fluctuations in temperature, fire and predators, both now and in the future. The main predator is the tuatara. A tuatara-proof fence has been constructed around the frogs' habitat. The Department of Conservation prohibits mammals being introduced to the island and limits visitors to its own staff and scientists.

The tuatara: the main predator of the Hamilton frog

Conclusion

Setting up a new colony of 40 frogs is recommended as soon as possible. The site selected is similar to that on Stephen's Island, with a rock stack and a forest over the top. The temperature and humidity of the new habitat have been monitored for the past two years, and have been found to be almost the same as on Stephen's Island.

Conrad's journal

Conrad Grieves is a scientist living on Stephen's Island to study the habits of Hamilton frogs.

Saturday

Estimate the wind to be about 140 kilometres an hour. Had to check frogs. Thought wind might help me walk quicker – held open my coat. Wind caught the coat like a sail on a boat – picked me up – flew at least 6 metres down the track.

Sunday

Very calm and sunny after storm. Spent evening fishing. Felt a sharp tug on the line – got very excited. Not a fish – a seal pup had swum off with the sinker. He dropped it after a bit and swam back. I could hear him sneaking up behind me. As soon as I turned around he lurched off. It was like playing 'What's the time, Mr Wolf?', especially when three of his friends joined in.

Monday

Great excitement – bulb in lighthouse blew! Had to ring lighthouse people in Wellington to talk me through how to shut down the system to stop the lights revolving. Changed the bulb, started up the system.

Wonder how the keeper managed in the 1890s – a guy called David Lyall, here on his own. Lyall acquired a cat for company that was all too successful at hunting. Apparently Tibbles caught a dozen tiny birds in one day – brought them home but didn't eat them.

Lyall noticed the birds were all the same species. Sent one to Wellington, describing the birds as flightless and running like mice. Identified as a new species of wren. By that time, Tibbles had killed all wrens on the island – made extinct by a cat! Tibbles also blamed for eradicating an entire species of lizard.

Tuesday

Six men arrived to plant native trees – no jetty or wharf here. Boat nudges up to the rocks – you have to jump and hope for the best. One missed, and went swimming. Waves choppy and water very cold – had to swim back to boat and try again. Made it on second attempt.

Searching for Dragon's Gold

Do YOU have the courage to seize the dragon's gold?

Take with you:
the map
food
waterproof clothes
a sleeping bag

a torch
a compass
a large rucksack

WARNING: Do not listen to anyone else along the way. The dragon's pet vulture can change shape — and will try to send you in the wrong direction.

Approach with CAUTION!

Dragon's Gate
Drago Mountains

Watch out for snakes!

The ruined hovel.
Strike out northwards through the thicket

Continue for 10 miles

Tarragon Forest

To Zoret

Mind the leeches!

Don't stray off the main path!

DANGER!

Bembly Cascade

Edge behind the waterfall to cross the river. Beware treacherous rocks underfoot.

Hide, watch and wait. The dragon goes hunting every third day. Move quickly and claim the gold for your own!

River Bembly

YOU ARE

HERE

← To Blimpford

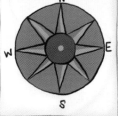

Head eastwards out of Blimpford.

1 MILE

Flying Carpet

PERSIAN MODEL RMX500 OPERATING INSTRUCTIONS

Before take-off

Unroll carpet carefully. Place near an open door or window. Allow at least 3 metres from breakable objects.

Place luggage in the centre and secure with luggage straps. (To locate luggage straps press gently in centre of carpet. Straps will pop out from points marked **X**.)

Seat passengers around edge of carpet. Balance weight evenly to ensure a smooth ride.

To operate

Note: The magic operating spell for your particular carpet will have arrived separately. NEVER store spells in the same place as magic transportation devices.

To operate, sit at point (**Y**). Ensure passengers are holding rings (**Z**) securely.

Grasp 'OPERATION' tassel (**O**) and turn 90° to the LEFT. Listen for the jingle. Recite operating spell clearly.

During the ascent you may experience a sudden juddering. This is normal.

Grasp the 'STAR-NAV' tassel (**SN**) and turn 90° to the RIGHT. Listen for the jingle. Speak your destination.

Hold tight. Take-off can be bumpy and may cause gastric disturbances.

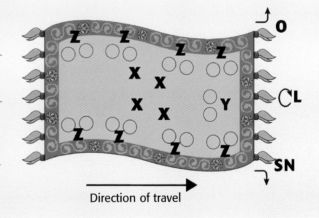

Direction of travel

During flight

A map will be projected in front of the carpet by the 'STAR NAV' tassel.

To steer, instruct passengers to lean left or right as required. In windy conditions, passengers should shuffle carefully towards centre of carpet to avoid being blown away.

Landing

When your destination appears on map, instruct passengers to adopt safety position ready for landing.

Turn 'LANDING' tassel (**L**) in a complete circle, clockwise. The carpet will complete its descent automatically. Have a safe flight.

Safety position for landing

ENJOY YOUR FLIGHTS WITH THE RMX500!

Amazing Journeys

Each year, 4,000 species of birds set out on an amazing journey. They leave one habitat and fly across the world to another, to get the best conditions for feeding and breeding. This journey is called migration.

Swallows mean summer

Swallows fly 10,000 km (6,000 miles) from South Africa to Britain in about 4 weeks. They arrive in the UK in early spring and breed. By September, they group together on telegraph wires and get ready to make the flight back to South Africa. They face many dangers and problems on the way. For example, they are shot at for sport by hunters in France. They are also preyed on by Eleanora falcons in the Mediterranean.

Swallows fly from South Africa to Britain in about 4 weeks

Small but strong

The willow warbler makes an amazing journey for such a tiny bird – it weighs about the same as a small box of matches. Each spring it flies about 8,000 km (5,000 miles) from West Africa to Britain and returns each autumn after the young have fledged.

Travelling alone

Ospreys, unlike many other birds, migrate alone. They spend the summer in northern England and Scotland and return to the warmer climate of West Africa in the autumn.

A willow warbler on the way to West Africa

The most amazing journey

The Arctic tern makes the longest migration of any living creature – in the air, on land or in the sea. It makes a round trip between northern Scotland or even the Arctic and the Antarctic, every year. This means a round trip of up to 35,000 km (22,000 miles). It arrives in Scotland or the Arctic to breed in May and early June and returns to the Antarctic between late July and early October.

When you've got to go …

All over the world, millions of birds migrate each year. They fly thousands of miles to get to a place with good conditions that will give them the best chance of survival.

Small birds get a signal to move from hormones in their body. This leads to an urge to feed, known as a 'feeding frenzy'. They must eat a lot so that they store as much fat as possible. The willow warbler uses this fat to get to Africa quickly. When its body weight is back to normal, the little bird knows it can stop flying.

Larger birds cannot store enough fat to make their migration journey non-stop because they would become too heavy to fly. The osprey takes two months to make its journey between the UK and Africa and stops at estuaries and lakes along the way so it can rest and eat fish.

An osprey stops for a snack

	length	weight	wingspan	duration of flight
Willow warbler	10½–11½ cm	7–12 g	16–22 cm	3 weeks
Swallow	17–20 cm	16–25 g	32–35 cm	4–6 weeks
Arctic tern	33–35 cm	95–120 g	70–80 cm	2–3 months
Osprey	50–60 cm	1120–2050 g	150–170 cm	2 months

UK visitors

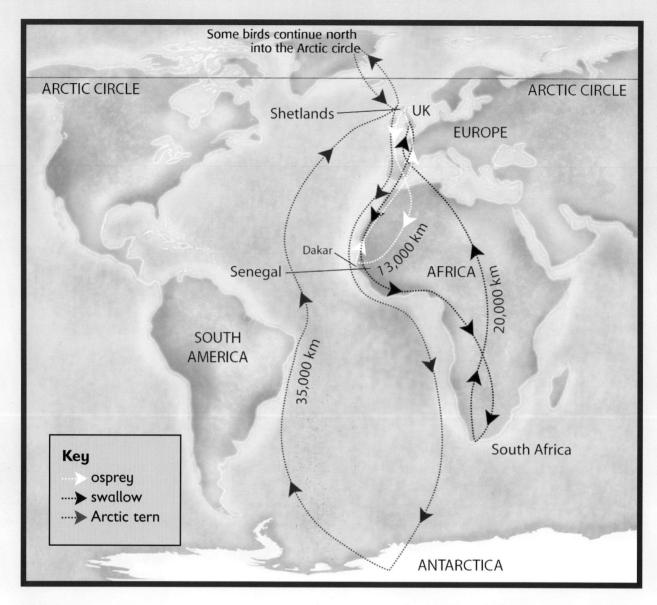

Some birds continue north into the Arctic circle

ARCTIC CIRCLE

ARCTIC CIRCLE

Shetlands

UK

EUROPE

Dakar

Senegal

13,000 km

AFRICA

20,000 km

SOUTH AMERICA

35,000 km

South Africa

Key
- osprey
- swallow
- Arctic tern

ANTARCTICA

Saving energy

Birds which migrate in groups fly in patterns which help them to use their energy most efficiently. They can fly up to 70% further when they fly like this.

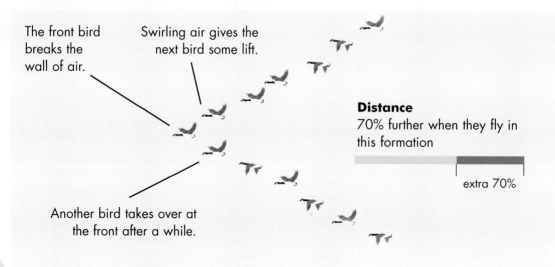

The front bird breaks the wall of air.

Swirling air gives the next bird some lift.

Another bird takes over at the front after a while.

Distance
70% further when they fly in this formation

extra 70%

Migration Marvels

When and how?

Many fish and marine animals migrate through the world's oceans. Some make an annual expedition. Others migrate only once – and then die.

They have different ways of navigating to their destinations. Salmon may be able to taste or smell their way back to the place where they first hatched. Scientists believe that whales and turtles can sense the direction and strength of the earth's magnetic field. However they manage to do it, migrating sea creatures have one thing in common: they all know the way.

To the sea – and back

Young salmon hatch out far upstream in rivers and immediately have an overwhelming urge to reach the sea. They spend half of their adult life feeding in the ocean and then begin the long journey back to the spawning grounds of very same river. Salmon do not feed in fresh water so they have lost around 40% of their body weight by the time they lay and fertilize their eggs. As a result, most of them die in the rivers and only a few return to the sea.

Salmon jump up waterfalls on their way to their spawning ground

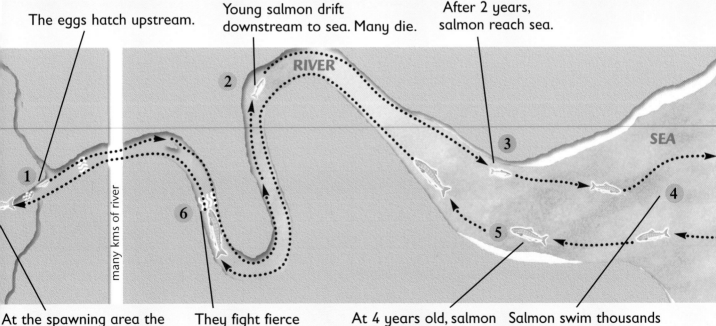

The eggs hatch upstream.

Young salmon drift downstream to sea. Many die.

After 2 years, salmon reach sea.

RIVER

SEA

many kms of river

At the spawning area the female lays her eggs. 95% of the salmon then die.

They fight fierce currents and jump waterfalls.

At 4 years old, salmon swim back to their breeding ground.

Salmon swim thousands of miles to ocean feeding ground.

Progress of salmon to the sea and back

The longest journey

Baleen whales have the longest migration of any mammal. They migrate in search of concentrations of tiny marine creatures, called plankton, to feed on.

Each species of whale has its own route. For example, the grey whale spends the summer feeding in the Arctic. When the ocean freezes, it migrates south down the coast of America to spend the winter in warmer water in Baja California and Costa Rica. The females give birth here. The whale calves feed on their mother's milk until they are 6–8 months old. They need to build up a layer of blubber (fat) to give them enough energy to migrate north with their family in the summer.

Grey whale calendar

J	F	M	A	M	J	J	A	S	O	N	D	J	F	M	A	M	J	J	A	S	O	N	D

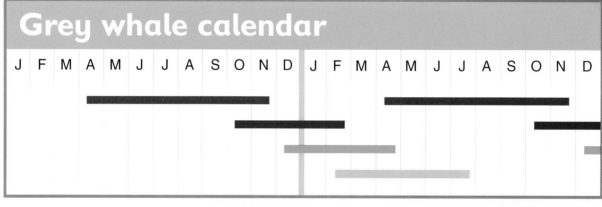

feed in cold Arctic waters ▬▬▬▬▬ breed in warm waters ▬▬▬▬▬

migrate south ▬▬▬▬▬ migrate north ▬▬▬▬▬

Turtle voyages

Turtles also make long journeys between feeding and breeding sites. Migration routes depend upon the species. Some leatherback turtles lay eggs in Costa Rica and make their way through a narrow corridor of sea to the Galapagos islands. Loggerhead turtles start their long journey when they are only 5 cm long. It takes them 5-10 years to complete the circuit back to their breeding beaches.

Loggerhead turtle

These amazing stories show how many creatures follow their species' natural urge to travel vast distances by sea to find the best location in order to survive. Although it is difficult to track their movements, scientists know that their routes are not determined by chance. However, there is still much to learn about migrations across the sea.

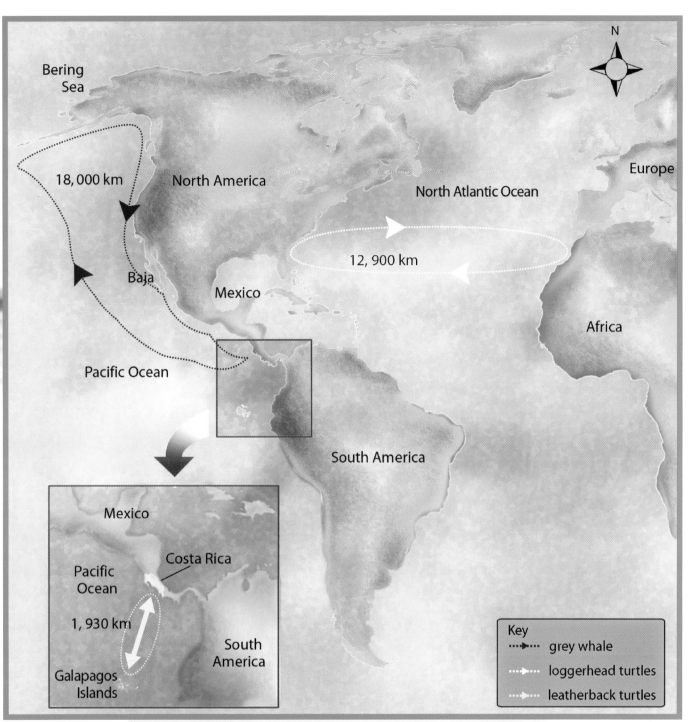

Map showing the long migration patterns of grey whale, loggerhead and leatherback turtles.

Bering Sea

18, 000 km

North America

North Atlantic Ocean

Europe

Baja

Mexico

12, 900 km

Africa

Pacific Ocean

South America

N

Key
····▶···· grey whale
····▶···· loggerhead turtles
····▶···· leatherback turtles

Mexico

Costa Rica

Pacific Ocean

1, 930 km

South America

Galapagos Islands

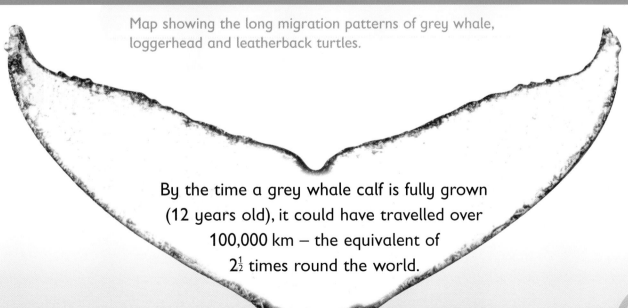

By the time a grey whale calf is fully grown (12 years old), it could have travelled over 100,000 km — the equivalent of $2\frac{1}{2}$ times round the world.

Transporting Water

Ancient methods

People living in areas where there was very little rainfall needed a system that would carry water to their crops. A machine called the **Archimedes Screw** was invented at least 2,000 years ago, to raise water from rivers to the higher land where it was used to irrigate crops.

Archimedes was a mathematician and inventor who lived in Sicily about 2,000 years ago.

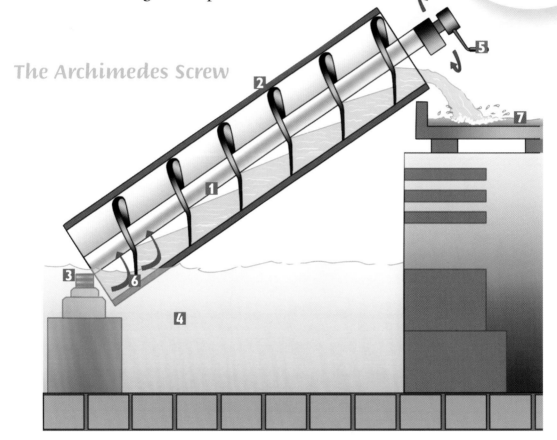

The Archimedes Screw

The machine is made up of a screw (1) inside a hollow pipe (2). One end of the pipe is submerged in water (3), usually a river or lake (4). The screw is then turned by a shaft handle (5). As the bottom of the screw turns, it scoops up water and carried it up the spiral (6) and finally, the water falls out from the top of the tube into a container or irrigation ditch (7).

A screw is a sloping surface wrapped around a cylinder, connecting a lower level to a higher level. Think of wrapping a length of cord around a pencil, from top to bottom.

Modern water towers

Modern methods

Water towers come in many shapes and sizes, but they all do the same thing: they provide water pressure which helps to get the water to where it is needed.

A water tower is simply a large tank of water. Gravity forces the water in the tank downwards and along a network of pipes to supply houses and businesses in the area.

The tank needs to be high up so that the water inside is under pressure. Then the water in the pipes will also be under pressure, and can supply a steady level of water pressure in the tap. So water towers are often very tall and are situated in hilly regions. In some areas, however, a tower might not be necessary. An ordinary tank located on the highest hill in the area might be able to supply enough pressure.

How a water tower works

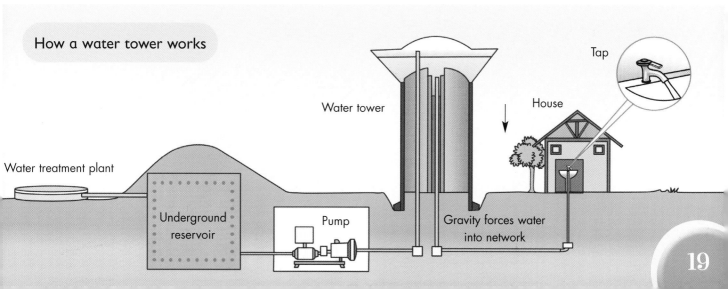

Water treatment plant

Water tower

Tap

House

Underground reservoir

Pump

Gravity forces water into network

Harnessing the Power of WATER

In the late 18th century, moving goods by horse-drawn road transport was costly. Using boats on slow-moving rivers was a cheaper and faster method. To increase the capacity of the water transport system, new canals were built. Boats have to travel along flat water, but the land rose and fell. Locks were built to carry boats between sections of canal at different levels.

How do canal locks work?

- At each end of the lock, there are heavy **gates** built of timber or steel.

- Openings (known as '**paddles**') are cut into the gates or the side of the lock. When the top paddles are opened, they let water into the lock from the higher stretch of canal, to raise the water level in the lock. When the bottom paddles are opened, they let water out and lower the water level in the lock.

- Each lock gate has a long '**balance beam**'. People push or pull the balance beam to open or close the gate and let the boat through.

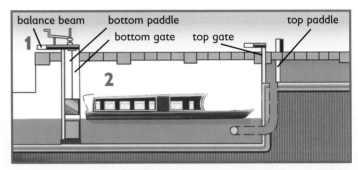

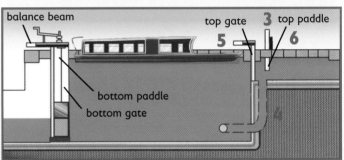

Going up

1. The bottom gate is opened by pushing the balance beam.
2. The boat sails into the lock and the bottom gate is closed.
3. The top gate paddles are opened.
4. Water flows into the lock from the upper level.
5. The water in the lock rises to the same level as the upper canal.
6. The top gate is opened and the boat can sail on.

To go down, the process is reversed, but opening the bottom gate paddles instead, to let water out of the lock and lower the boat.

How were canal tunnels built?

It wasn't always possible to build locks to go over large hills, so tunnels were needed to take the canal through some hills.

1. A straight route was marked out across the hill.

2. A number of shafts were dug.

3. Digging began in both directions from the bottom of the shafts. All excavation was done by pickaxe, shovel and gunpowder, making progress slow and laborious.

Canal boats were originally powered by horse. The horse walked along the towpath beside the canal, towing the boat on a rope. Few early tunnels had towpaths. So how did canal boats get through tunnels?

The horse was unhitched and led over the hill and the boat was 'legged' through the tunnel. Two people (known as 'leggers') lay on planks hanging over the side of the boat, and 'walked' their feet along the tunnel wall to propel the boat along.

Tunnels were left in a natural state where the rock was solid, or arched with brick or stone where the rock strata were weak.

A modern canal

Leggers

The Joys of Being a Victorian Child

Some people today think it was no fun to be a child in Queen Victoria's time. They say life then was slow and really rather dull. No one can deny that Victorian children lived in a very different world from ours. True, poor children had to go out to work very young. Some of them may well have fallen ill or died doing filthy jobs in factories or sweeping chimneys. But even so, no one had to work all the time – and there were ways for even the poorest Victorian child to have a lot of fun.

Queen Victoria, who reigned from 1837 to 1901, knew all about children: she had nine of her own!

Life on the street

Where did these poor children play? Anywhere they liked – including the streets right outside their homes, since there was no motor traffic. You must agree it would be fun not to have to dodge cars all the time. They could also roam around freely in gangs, without their parents feeling they had to check up on them all the time.

But what was there to do on the streets? For a few pennies, children could buy cheap wooden dolls or tin whistles from street sellers. For no cost at all they made their own footballs out of rags. Children made their own music too, playing street singing games like 'Have You Seen The Muffin Man?', accompanying themselves, no doubt, on their tin whistles.

Children from richer families had upstairs nurseries to play in rather than the street. Their parents could afford flashier toys: beautifully-dressed dolls, rocking horses – or even real horses for them to ride (although not in the nursery!). They had amazing new children's books too, like Lewis Carroll's *Alice in Wonderland* and the Fairy Tales of Hans Christian Andersen. Just imagine being the first person in your class to get to read one of those.

Sunday play

It's true that people went to church a lot in Victorian times, and children were supposed to show respect to God by not playing much on Sundays.

This event must have gone well – they've been holding Cup Finals ever since!

Stuff and nonsense

Some people think Victorian children's books were dull and serious. As you can see from his poem and picture, Victorian author Edward Lear wouldn't agree.

There was an Old Man on whose nose
Most birds of the air could repose;
But they all flew away
At the closing of day,
Which relieved that Old Man and his nose.

Don't get the impression that church was boring. Many churches had sports clubs for young people. That was how Everton and Aston Villa football clubs got started in Liverpool and Birmingham.

In Victorian times really lucky children might be taken along to watch top sports stars in action. Test Match cricket was just taking off, and so were the Wimbledon tennis championships and professional golf tournaments – and of course there was top-class football. Wanderers beat the Royal Engineers by a single goal to win the first English FA Cup Final of 1872 in front of a crowd of 2,000 people. At that time there were still no crossbars or nets on the goals. So you had to watch very closely to see that goal being scored!

Full steam ahead!

Everyone knows how exciting it is when new things come in. For thousands of years if you wanted to travel overland quickly you had to use horses, and horses weren't cheap. Then along came speedy steam trains. It must have seemed like a miracle.

Be honest – wouldn't you have loved to swim in privacy from a Victorian horse-drawn 'bathing machine' like this one?

It meant that even quite poor children could go on long journeys. Some rode all the way to the coast with their families to enjoy holidays at new resorts like Blackpool, Margate and Brighton.

And the exciting novelties did not stop there. You have to hand it to those Victorians – they knew how to dream up fun things at the seaside. You name it, the Victorians invented it: Punch and Judy shows on the beach, donkey rides, buckets and spades, ice creams in cornets, takeaway fish and chips. They even invented the first cameras, so you could have your photo taken on holiday – photos that prove to us just how much fun those Victorian kids could have!

Question

Why didn't Victorian children get much of a tan at the seaside?

(a) Because it sometimes wasn't sunny enough.

(b) Because it was more fashionable to have milky white skin in those days.

(c) Because Victorian swimwear kept most of your flesh 'decently' covered up so that God was not offended.

Answer: All of the above!

Do the Ancient Greeks Still Matter?

What do you think about History? Is it worth thinking about it at all? Surely it's more sensible to concentrate on the here and now, and look ahead rather than back? Well, some bits of History aren't just dead and buried. Certain people in History – like the Ancient Greeks – had such a big effect that they just won't go away. It's as if their spirit has continued to live on until today, sometimes in ways you really would not have expected…

Olympic class people

Go back a thousand years, then another thousand, then almost *another* thousand. The pyramids of Egypt were then quite new. Neither Jesus Christ nor the prophet Mohammed had yet been born. But in the Mediterranean region, something special was happening. The people we now call the Ancient Greeks were busily creating their own little world. These Greeks were some of the cleverest, most creative and highly civilised people who ever walked the Earth.

Their world lasted for just a few centuries, then the mighty Romans took most of it over. But the Greeks left a lot behind: great art, great buildings – and great books that tell us how they lived and what amazing, ahead-of-their-time ideas they had. These ideas were not just about things like science, medicine and politics. The Greeks were also just as obsessed with sport and physical exercise as we are. Everyone knows about the four-yearly Olympic Games today. You may be surprised to learn it was the Greeks who started them up, way back in 776 BC.

The Greeks were people of action too. In a series of wars soon after 500 BC they overcame enormous odds to defeat armies of invaders from the powerful Persian empire. If you think you have built up a great civilization, then you have to be prepared to fight for it – and the Greeks did both!

The Greeks may have believed in some odd things – they were very superstitious – but they certainly knew how to hold a celebration. Those Ancient Greek Olympic Games were part of a big religious festival, for instance.

No one is saying the Greeks were perfect. It's a fact that they used slaves, and that girls and women didn't get as many chances in life as boys and men. But you can't help but be impressed by their thirst for knowledge. Many modern subjects like botany and philosophy have Greek names because the Greeks either invented them or made big contributions to them. In many ways they set the ball rolling for us. Modern doctors, for example, still study the symptoms of illnesses in the way suggested by Hippocrates the Ancient Greek.

You don't have to go to a museum or read a history book to check out the Ancient Greeks – they're still all around you. Many Greek buildings lasted for centuries, and inspired later architects to copy them.

Hippocrates: the Father of Medicine

A town hall near you may well have columns with carved tops, just like the Greeks made for their places of worship.

Things can only get better?

You might think people in the past can't have done things as well as we do. Yet is that always true? Look at the Ancient Greek statues on this page. You have to admit they're so good, they take your breath away. Generations of later sculptors have modelled their own work on them – and often failed to equal them.

In the same way, could a modern fantasy writer (even the creator of Harry Potter!) equal the Ancient Greek *Odyssey* for excitement, horror and just plain weirdness? Homer's classic story has inspired countless later authors at least to try. You can see why the Ancient Greeks felt superior to other peoples of their time – and why they called them all 'barbarians', or 'babblers of total nonsense'!

What's in a name?

And have you ever heard of a Thea or an Alexander, a Sophie or a Jason, a Philip or a Phoebe? You might even have heard of a Homer, or a Hermione… All those names echo down to us from Ancient Greek history, poems, myths and legends. (In the gym you may have run up against the name Nike. She was an Ancient Greek goddess of victory!)

Hercules fights the Hydra on a pot from 2000 years ago – as he still does in modern-day cartoons and films!

Take the Greeks' word for it

We still retell and make films of Greek tales like the siege of Troy and the labours of Hercules. Greek myths are full of dragons and monsters you won't find in any zoo! And modern theatres put on plays that were written by Greek authors over 2,000 years ago – translated into modern English, of course!

It's as if the Greeks lit a lamp and its warm red glow still lights our way today. You don't believe that? Well, just look at all the English words highlighted on this page. Every one comes from Ancient Greek. And even new words like telephone and photograph are made from old Greek words. There really is no getting away from those absolutely great Ancient Greeks!

Writing the Dictionary

The idea for a dictionary containing every word in the English language was thought of in 1857 by the Philological Society. They thought it would take about 10 years to write. In fact it took nearly 70 years!

The plan was that the dictionary should not just explain the words, but should also say where each word came from, and how its meaning had changed over the years. This meant finding examples of how every word had been used at different times in history. It was a huge task. When James Murray took over the project in 1879, he realised that a lot of help was needed so he issued an appeal, inviting people to send in slips of paper, giving the word they found and a quotation from the book where they found it, showing how it was used.

Within a year, hundreds of people had sent in more than 360,000 slips, and they all had to be sorted. Murray employed a team of assistants – and his eleven children.

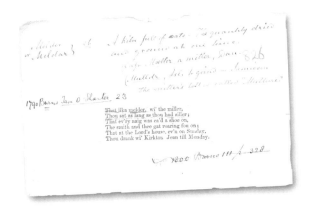

An original OED wordslip

As soon as they were old enough to read, the children earned their pocket money by sorting the slips into alphabetical order, starting at a penny an hour.

Murray had a corrugated iron shed built in his garden, where work on the dictionary took place. He called this office his 'Scriptorium'. It was lined with more than a thousand pigeonholes, so the slips could be kept in order. Sorting them was only the start – next, the team had to write definitions for every word!

It took nearly 70 years, but when the Oxford English Dictionary was finally published in 1928, it contained 252,200 words, 1.8 million quotations, and filled 10 huge books.

Murray and his family

Murray did, with the
at if the glue didn't stick?...

trance NOUN

he way into a place

trance VERB

lift VERB

1 raise or pick up something.
2 rise or go upwards.
3 remove or abolish something –
The ban has been lifted.

screen VERB

1 protect, hide, or divide with a screen.
2 show a film or television
pictures on a screen.

log NOUN

2 a detailed record kept of a
voyage or flight.

4 (informal) steal.

fill with intense delight

1 a large piece of a tree that
has fallen or been cut
down; a piece cut off this.

follow closely or persistently –
Reporters dogged his footsteps.

3 rest against something.
4 rely or depend on someone
for help.

3 carry out tests on someone to
find out if they have a disease.
4 check whether a person is
suitable for a job.

29

The Dictionary-makers

In 1857, the Philological Society decided to create an innovative, comprehensive dictionary of the English language. It would include every English word, and not just explain what the words meant, but describe their history too, to show how meanings had changed over time.

For the first 20 years, progress was slow. A new editor, James Murray, took over the project in 1879 and swiftly made a public appeal for help.

He asked people to find as many different uses of English words as possible, from books in English through the ages. Soon, thousands of words and quotations started arriving, all written or pasted on individual slips of paper.

Minor's minuscule notes – at actual size!

Some people contributed huge numbers of these slips. One such volunteer was Dr William Chester Minor, an inmate at Broadmoor Asylum for the Criminally Insane. Some say that the widow of the man he had murdered brought him some library books, one of which had Murray's appeal leaflet tucked inside. Whether that's true or not, what is certain is that Minor began to catalogue the words in every book he read, on small sheets of paper, in tiny handwriting. He amassed such a vast collection of antiquarian books that he was granted the use of the room adjacent to his own, to use as a study. Over 21 years, he supplied more than 12,000 quotations for the dictionary.

Once the slips had been sorted into alphabetical order, the lexicographers wrote definitions for the words. J.R.R. Tolkien, who became famous for writing 'The Hobbit' and 'The Lord of the Rings', worked on words beginning with 'w', a particularly difficult group because it includes the oldest words in the English language.

Language is always changing, and the Oxford English Dictionary still depends on people sending in examples of new words. Once a word goes into the OED, it's never removed, so the editors wait for 10 years, to check that a word really is in use, before including it in the next update.

Word-making

Many English words come from Greek and Latin words. It's like cracking a code – if you know what the Greek or Latin word means, you can work out what the English word must mean. For example, once you know that 'hydro' means water, can you guess what conditions a hydrangea plant likes? Or what a hydrant might be? Or what source of power a hydraulic device uses?

Some English words are made up of Greek or Latin words put together. Look at the words in these boxes. You might know what a centipede is, but what does its name actually mean? What about a millipede, or a submarine, or a photograph? You might even be able to work out what a lexicographer does! You can invent your own words by putting bits together. Who knows – they might even make it into the dictionary one day!

WORD beginnings

agora = market place; open space
anthropos = human being
arachnid = spider
auto = self
bio = life
bronchus = windpipe
centi = hundred
co = together
eco = to do with the environment
hemi = half
hydro = water
hypo = under, below
inter = between
lexis = word
mega = large
micro = small
milli = thousand
omni = everything
philo = love
photo = light
sub = under
tele = far

WORD endings

gradus = a step
graphy = writing
itis = inflammation
logos = word
marine = sea
ology = study
ordinate = arrange
pedes = feet
philia = love
phobia = fear
phone = voice
potent = able, strong
terra = ground
thermia = temperature

Pardon?

I've got a touch of bronchitis so I only have a hemiphone today.

Index